FAMILY VACATION FEEDBACK CARD

Do you wish to remain anonymous?
☐ Yes ☐ No ☐ Yes, but then have my name leaked during the holidays

Please share my feedback:
☐ With immediate family only ☐ In the extended family newsletter
☐ With the mainstream media ☐ With the police

How would you rate your overall experience of the vacation?
☐ Very poor ☐ Poor ☐ OK ☐ Good ☐ Very good ☐ Damaging
☐ The repercussions haven't sunk in yet ☐ Absolutely no recollection
☐ I can't feel my legs ☐ Don't know ☐ Dull

We all agreed upon returning home that this vacation had some truly memorable moments. Which were your favorites? (Please check all that apply)
☐ That authentic Albanian restaurant ☐ The windy walk along the cliff
☐ Getting rid of the hitchhiker ☐ That quality moment of Wi-Fi
☐ Discovering why the whole family stammers ☐ Braking in the nick of time
☐ Faking a seizure midflight to get upgraded

Any others? Please provide specific examples of what you did or did not enjoy.

_____

What elements could have improved the vacation?
☐ Less broken glass on the beach ☐ Sex ☐ Fewer churches
☐ Private room ☐ Roofed house ☐ Solid food ☐ Proper map
☐ Spare tire ☐ Fighting fire with fire ☐ More/less crime ☐ Own spoon

Other elements? Please specify: _____

Think back to previous vacations. Did you enjoy the following locations more or less than the last one? (M = more, L = less)
☐ Fargo ☐ South China Sea ☐ Disney World knockoff ☐ Emotional Purgatory
☐ The demilitarized zone ☐ Los Angeles ☐ Paris sewer ☐ Appalachian Trail
☐ Attic ☐ Judith's "World of Botanics" ☐ Abandoned oil rig ☐ Somali Coast
☐ Car trunk

Is there anyone you would prefer not to go on the family vacation with next time?
☐ Mother ☐ Father ☐ Father's girlfriend ☐ Sister ☐ Brother
☐ Aunt ☐ Racist aunt ☐ Harmonica-playing cousin ☐ Sommelier uncle
☐ Quiet uncle ☐ Mother's friend "having a tough time" ☐ Mother's "friend"
☐ My girlfriend and/or boyfriend ☐ That strange former army major ☐ Pet fish

FAMILY DINNER FEEDBACK CARD

Food

Overall the food was:

☐ Average ☐ Soooo average ☐ Good
☐ Excellent ☐ Needs improvement
☐ Prefer other family's meals (If so, please specify other family: _____)

How would you describe the portions?

☐ Too small ☐ Just right
☐ Too large ☐ Wartime ☐ Punitive
☐ Irrelevant (couldn't keep it down)
☐ Fine, but prefer separate soup and dessert bowls

Please rate the cuisine on the following spectrums: (Circle a number from 1 to 5)

Bland	1	2	3	4	5	Spicy
Tart	1	2	3	4	5	Cynical
Soft	1	2	3	4	5	Painfully hard
Green	1	2	3	4	5	Brown
Windy	1	2	3	4	5	Feverish
Salty	1	2	3	4	5	Sobering
Sweet	1	2	3	4	5	Cheeky

Do you have any dietary preferences that weren't taken into account this time?

☐ Vegetarian ☐ Low sodium
☐ Set in my ways ☐ On hunger strike
☐ Vegan ☐ Gluten-free
☐ Pumpkin-skeptic ☐ Seed-conscious
☐ No appendix ☐ General prejudice
☐ Penicillin allergy ☐ Can't digest hair
☐ _____ -intolerant (please specify allergen)

Service

Overall the service was:

☐ Average ☐ Good ☐ Excellent
☐ Needs Improvement
☐ Disciplinary action necessary

Which words best describe the service you received?

☐ Slow ☐ Fast ☐ Rushed
☐ Friendly ☐ Lacked flair
☐ Poignant ☐ Heavy-handed
☐ Server born for the role
☐ Server allowed personal feelings to influence work
☐ N/A (Meal was self-service)

Ambience & Socializing

Overall the ambience was:

☐ Average ☐ Good ☐ Excellent
☐ Prefer lights on
☐ Elephant in the room too overwhelming
☐ Elephant in the room adorable

The doctor's presence:

☐ Added to proceedings
☐ Spoiled things ☐ Was sexy
☐ Was unnoticed

I thought the music was:

☐ Pleasant ☐ Tahitian ☐ Live
☐ Difficult to sing along to

I found the conversation:

☐ Entirely appropriate ☐ Too medical
☐ Difficult in so many languages

The speaking time allotment was:

☐ Stressful ☐ Helpful ☐ Essential

THE YEAR IN REVIEW

The Year Two Thousand and _____ was one of the:
- [ ] Best [ ] Longest [ ] Highest in saturated fats [ ] Most uneventful and rainy
- [ ] Most intriguing [ ] Haziest [ ] Most nightmarish and sadistically unending
- [ ] Most joy filled [ ] Most agrarian [ ] Last [ ] _____

It was filled with:
- [ ] Memorable train journeys [ ] Hilarious episodes of self-endangerment
- [ ] Questionable masseurs [ ] Exciting divorces [ ] Exercise
- [ ] Experimental diets [ ] Tom Cruise [ ] Comic neuroses [ ] New religions
- [ ] Wisdom from our leaders [ ] The predictably unpredictable
- [ ] Blossoming marigolds [ ] Winter [ ] Monkeys
- [ ] The unbearable lightness of being…right, always [ ] _____

Even while it lacked:
- [ ] Cheese [ ] Drama [ ] A sense that someone was in control [ ] Good manners
- [ ] Quality [ ] Results [ ] A good conspiracy theory [ ] Uncontaminated legumes
- [ ] New hip-hop artists [ ] A proper spring [ ] More than one sexual partner
- [ ] A trip to Gettysburg [ ] Individual pillows [ ] Resolution [ ] Continuity
- [ ] Animatronic pigeons [ ] A certain *je ne sais quoi* [ ] _____

Above all, it has solidified my belief that:
- [ ] Life is terrifying without you, or at least someone that looks very much like you
- [ ] Age is an illusion, albeit an incredibly convincing one
- [ ] Nudism is coming back
- [ ] Our neighbors are probably murderers but still excellent catsitters
- [ ] You *can* have your cake and eat it, but then regurgitate it
- [ ] My beekeeping got out of hand
- [ ] I should've researched Greenland more before our trip
- [ ] _____

How would you rate the year on the following spectrums?
(Circle a number from 1 to 10)

Pain	1 2 3 4 5 6 7 8 9 10	Gain
Sorrow	1 2 3 4 5 6 7 8 9 10	Gardening
Swimming	1 2 3 4 5 6 7 8 9 10	Pottery
Urban	1 2 3 4 5 6 7 8 9 10	Turban
Hips	1 2 3 4 5 6 7 8 9 10	Lips
Music	1 2 3 4 5 6 7 8 9 10	Weightlifting
Cooking	1 2 3 4 5 6 7 8 9 10	Crime

ANNUAL EMPLOYMENT SELF-REVIEW

How long have you been in your current position?

☐ **One week** ☐ **One month** ☐ **One year** ☐ **Two years** ☐ **Three years or more**
☐ **I don't know anymore**

How well are you able to repress the complete pointlessness of what you're doing?

☐ **Very well** ☐ **Not that well** ☐ **Wednesdays are the hardest**
☐ **My high-risk behavior speaks for itself**

What would be the best way to explain your occupation?

☐ **Information worker** ☐ **General liaison** ☐ **IT attaché** ☐ **In-house consultant**
☐ **Social climber** ☐ **Abstract attendee** ☐ **Importer/Exporter**
☐ **Bathroom visionary** ☐ **Horizon manager**

If you could change one thing about your boss, what would it be?

☐ **Nose** ☐ **Thyroid** ☐ **Sunglasses indoors** ☐ **Plumbing skills** ☐ **Stupid face**
☐ **The moments of his/her humanity that puncture my sense of righteous contempt**

The area in which I feel I'm doing best is:

☐ **My communication skills** ☐ **Circling back** ☐ **Walking around and cleaning up**
☐ **Stealing communal milk**

The area in which I think I could improve is:

☐ **Covering up my affair with a coworker** ☐ **Public speaking** ☐ **Blackmail**
☐ **Chewing pens**

Please rate how you think you're performing on the following spectrums:
(Circle a number from 1 to 10)

Being on the same page	1 2 3 4 5 6 7 8 9 10	**Not spoiling the ending**
Networking	1 2 3 4 5 6 7 8 9 10	**Not working**
Feedback	1 2 3 4 5 6 7 8 9 10	**Madness**
Open door policy	1 2 3 4 5 6 7 8 9 10	**Security problems**
Brainstorming	1 2 3 4 5 6 7 8 9 10	**Resting brain**
Management	1 2 3 4 5 6 7 8 9 10	**Nipple-clamps**
This was not what I intended	1 2 3 4 5 6 7 8 9 10	**This will have to do**

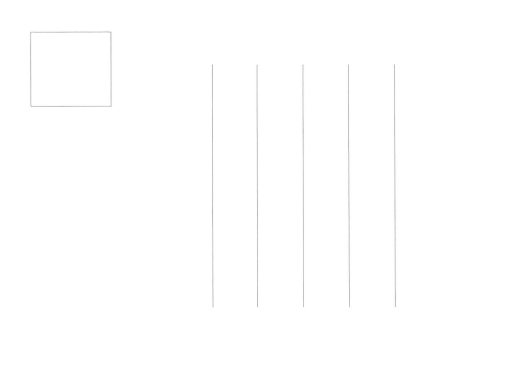

HOLIDAY FEEDBACK CARD

Please complete the sentence in a way that most accurately reflects how you felt over the holiday: "I think we can agree that this holiday…"

☐ Mistakes were made ☐ Was unnecessarily toxic ☐ Would have been better in Italy
☐ Was complicated by the "5 turkeys for the price of 4" deal
☐ Helped solve that missing person case ☐ "Merry" didn't even come into it

What was the best thing about this holiday?

☐ The calm ☐ Feeling of no demands ☐ All being together on our phones
☐ Our aunt being too frail to make her "famous" steamed squash
☐ Opening presents and guessing how much they cost
☐ Imagining where else I could be

What was the most problematic part of the holiday?

☐ The "uncle" who joined ☐ The freezer filled with fish and the power outage
☐ Choosing films based on the assistant director ☐ Freudian slips
☐ Backseat driving ☐ Confusing "presence" with "presents"
☐ Cake and "couscoustard"

Please rate your enjoyment of this year's holiday games on a scale of 1 to 10.

So you think you know Grandpa?   1 2 3 4 5 6 7 8 9 10

Long-buried family secrets revealed through charades   1 2 3 4 5 6 7 8 9 10

What would we change about our childhoods?   1 2 3 4 5 6 7 8 9 10

Gravy boat ultimate laxatives challenge   1 2 3 4 5 6 7 8 9 10

Strip Monopoly   1 2 3 4 5 6 7 8 9 10

My plate of food looks like Stalin!   1 2 3 4 5 6 7 8 9 10

The holiday was also a religious occasion—please indicate which of the following elements best celebrated its spiritual aspect:

☐ Toilet dressed like Santa ☐ Tears of blood emerging from the toast
☐ Sinfully indulgent pudding ☐ Princess Margaret Ouija board
☐ Singing hymns during *Gravy boat ultimate laxatives challenge*

Please circle which words describe your presents most accurately:

Practical	**Insomnia-inducing**	**Passive-aggresive**	**Last-minute**
Fun	**Shameful**	**Life-threatening**	**For the landfill**

I ☐ LOVE YOU ☐ HATE YOU

My _____ ,

I _____ you. I do.

I have this _____ feeling whenever I think
about you: at night, in the _____ , and in the
_____ , actually, especially in the _____ .

The very sound of your voice makes me feel
_____ . And your smell? It instantly fills me
with _____ .

I haven't been able to find the _____ to tell you
this before. But it's become impossible to _____ .

I have to tell you, and I have to tell you now:
I _____ you. I _____ you.
I just _____ you.

I implore you to _____ , so that I can sleep
again at night.

This is a lot to tell you. I hope it's _____ to hear.
Because know this: I want to see you _____ .

Then, and only then, can I be happy.

YOUR PARTY WAS ☐ GREAT ☐ LIKE TORTURE

Dear _____ ,

What a night! _____ **you for asking me to
your** _____ **party. The** _____ ,
the _____ , **and the** _____ **were all
completely** _____ . **It was truly** _____
to meet such _____ **people. And the**
_____ **? Completely** _____ **!**

**I only hope that one day I can host you at my own
home and** _____ **you to a similar level of**
_____ . **Of course, it seems almost impossible
that I'd be able to—you are pretty much unrivaled
when it comes to throwing** _____ **parties, as
last night again proved.**

I look forward to any future occasion with
_____ .

Yours,

_____

**P.S. By the way, can you please make sure that
I have** _____ **'s contact information so I
can ensure we** _____ **meet again? I want to
be able to** _____ **them on email. Thanks!**

YOU'RE BEING ☐ PROMOTED ☐ FIRED

To _____ ,

In recognition of your _____ performance this year, it gives me great pleasure to tell you that you're being _____ , effective immediately.

If I seem gleeful, I am. From the moment I became your supervisor, I knew you were destined to be _____ . You're too _____ an employee to stay in your current position—everyone can see that. Every move you've made at this company has resulted in _____ , and management has noticed.

With your new circumstances, I am sure that you _____ be able to afford that _____ you're always talking about—your family will be _____ .

This evening, I hope you'll have plenty of drinks to _____ with your coworkers, many of whom you may not see again. It'll be a mixed blessing if you wake up the next day hungover, as you'll have _____ else to be that day. Life's tough at the _____ !

Just remember—you've only been here for _____ and managed to be _____ in that time. A sign of things to come, no doubt. You _____ be missed! And I can't wait to see where you end up.

Yours sincerely,

_____

I AM ☐ SORRY ☐ NOT SORRY

Dear _____ ,

I've been thinking about it, I understand your criticism, and I've decided that an apology is _____ appropriate.

You _____ deserve it.

I've given this a lot of consideration, and I feel completely _____ at how I treated you. The way I behaved was _____ , and I look back on it with _____ .

Life is full of moral grays, and sometimes it's hard to tell right from wrong. In this case, however, I am unequivocal: I was _____ , and in the future I fully intend to behave _____ .

One more thing: as a token of how I feel about this whole incident, I've sent you a _____ of _____ . You should be receiving it very shortly.

Enjoy.

Yours,

_____

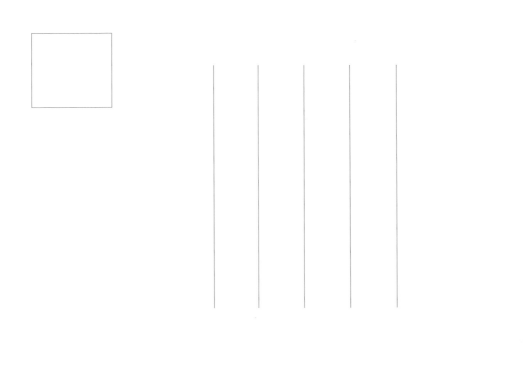

OFFICIAL WARNING

I'm warning you, officially.

You've done something wrong,
and I need you to know it.

OK, maybe it's really an
accumulation of small things.

But it's driven me to this.

I must send a signal.

I'm showing you a yellow card.

You have been warned.

I hope you noticed.

YOU ARE
DISMISSED

That's it. You're done.

I want—no, I *need*—you to leave.

You crossed a line and you can't
come back from it.

Not now.

I just can't believe you.

I even warned you with that yellow card.

It must have just looked like a
block of color to you.

Well, notice this red card. You're off.

What comes next, we'll have to see.

YOU'RE LOOKING TERRIFIC

Wow.

You look wonderful!

Is it the hair? No, you changed it
weeks ago, of course.

Sorry, I should have noticed.

Well, whatever it is,
your appearance is transformed.

No, that's not what I mean—
of course you always look great.

But it's like the lighting on you
has suddenly changed, or something.

WE NEED TO CHANGE OUR LIVES SOMEHOW

This won't do, not any more.

The gray days are starting to
outnumber the blue.

And I have this feeling, more often than not,
that we need to do something new—
build something or break something.

Maybe we should move.

Remember the pictures of that place
I showed you?

Actually, no—I think I'd enjoy the journey
to get fresh water.

The walk would be a pleasure.

FINANCES ARE IN TERRIBLE SHAPE

Sit—sit for a minute. No, leave the light off.

You're right.

The things you've noticed, they haven't
just been coincidences.

I haven't been stealing food "for fun."

There *is* a reason I won't let you
see the mail.

That man who's been ringing—
he means business.

And I think I've tried everything,
thought of everything, tried everyone.

My life insurance? I still have it.

No, it doesn't cover it. I already checked.

But yours does.

I'M
FINE

JUST GET

ON WITH YOUR

OWN LIFE

ABSOLUTELY

NOTHING

TO

WORRY ABOUT

YES

THAT

HAS DONE

LASTING

DAMAGE

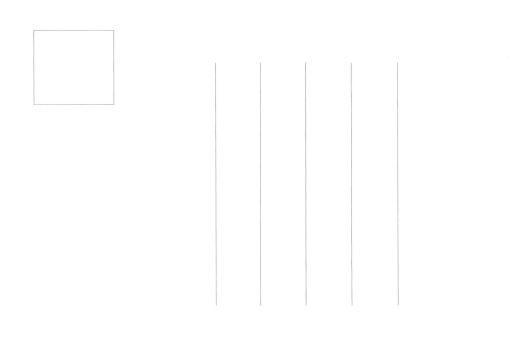

STOP

HAVEN'T YOU DONE ENOUGH

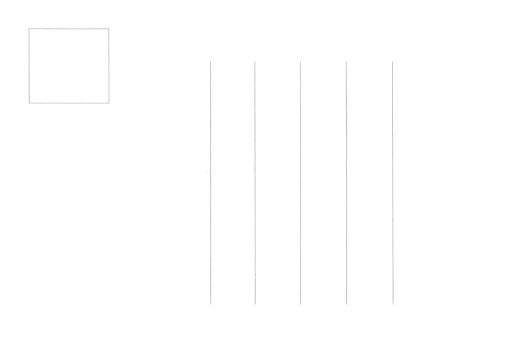

CELEBRATE

YOUR WORK

HERE

IS DONE

DEFINITELY

NOTHING

GOING ON

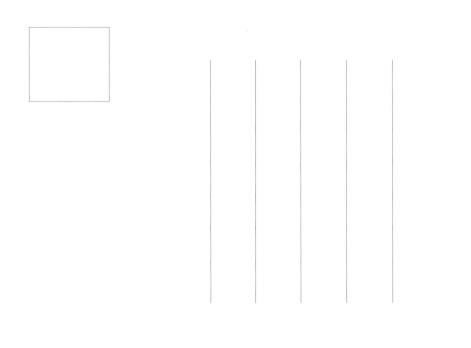

FYI

I'VE JUST
CROSSED
A THRESHOLD

JE NE REGRETTE RIEN

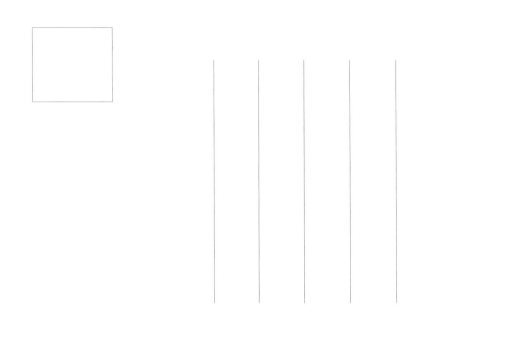

TODAY

IT'S ON A

KNIFE-EDGE

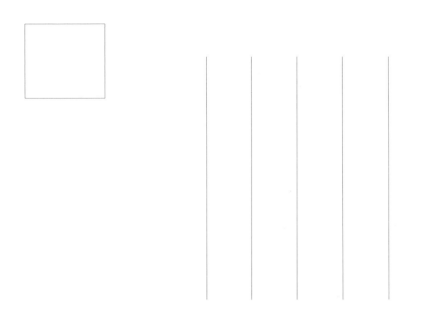

THIS

IS NOT

HOW I

IMAGINED

SATURDAY

DON'T
STRESS
ABOUT
LUNCH

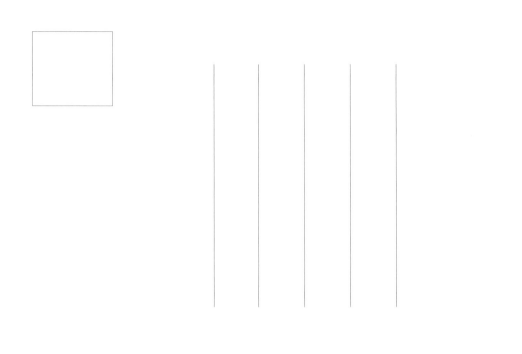

WHATEVER
IT IS
YOU DECIDE

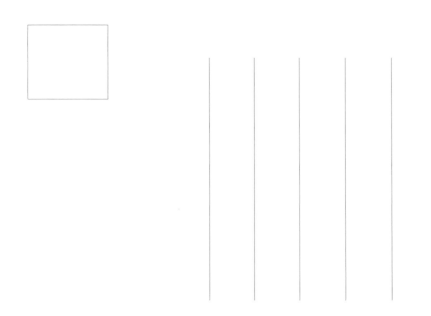

TURN BACK

IT'S

POINTLESS

ACT

AS IF

THERE'S

NOTHING

WRONG

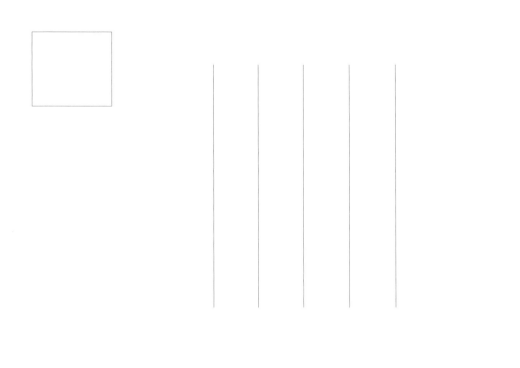

I

DON'T

MISS

MY

OLD LIFE

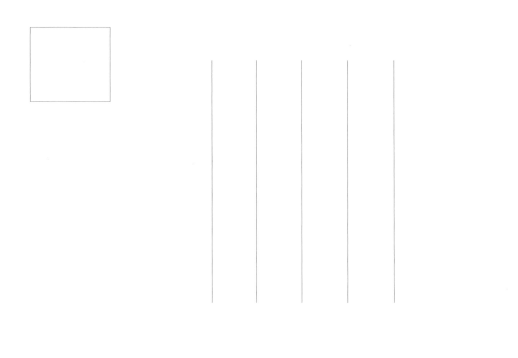

From Everything is Easy, published by
Princeton Architectural Press